AMERICAN MINING RIGHTS ASSOCIATION

Mining Act of 1872

Edited by M. Fernandez

*****

Editor's Note: In the 21st century, miners across this land are under fire like never before. We face extreme environmental groups, naive lawmakers, and out of control state and federal agencies.

As I study the issues facing miners, I realize a lot of misinformation and expired truths are being used against us.

Did our forefathers in the mining fields make huge mistakes and scar the land? Yes.
Did our forefathers in the mining fields use mercury to separate gold from sand and gravel and leave it in our waterways? Yes.

But miners today are a different breed. We have a passion for conservation not always understood by the average person. Our livelihoods are dependent on the land and we take care of it.

Miners actually remove other people's trash, lead, and mercury from waterways, their claims, and more. Most don't toot their own horns, preferring to quietly do the right thing with no applause.

*Let's not forget a very important fact; **mineral mining is necessary.** If not for these minerals being pulled from the earth, technology (and our very lives) would not be what they are today.*

Fine jewelry, 100% dependent on mining, would not even be available if not for mines and miners; men and women willing to risk their lives to extract the pretty things so many adorn themselves with.

Cell phones, flat screen televisions, automobiles, appliances, and more, would not be possible if not for miners who extract necessary minerals from the earth.

To attack miners for what we do is akin to attacking farmers for raising the foods we eat every day. It makes no sense.

In 1872, our leaders understood miners to be a valuable part of our nation's fabric. These forward thinking people saw a need for us and their desire was to secure our future.

How much more valuable we are today!

But our future is under fire.

Editor

These comments and views are my own

Mining Act of 1872

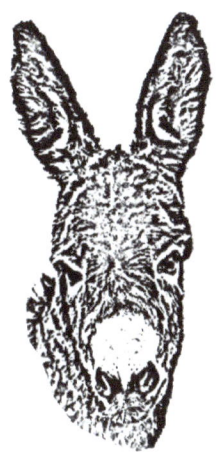

"An act to promote the development of the mining resources of the United States."

THE TEXT OF THE MINERS ACT OF 1872

Be it enacted by the Senate and House of Representatives of the United States of America in Congress assembled, That all valuable mineral deposits in lands belonging to the United States, both surveyed and unsurveyed, are hereby declared to be free and open to exploration and purchase, and the the lands in which they are found to occupation and purchase, by citizens of the United States and those who have declared their intention to become such, under regulations prescribed by law, and according to the local customs or rules of miners, in the several mining-districts, so far as the same are applicable and not inconsistent with the laws of the United States.

SEC. 2. That mining-claims upon veins or lodes of quartz or other rock in place bearing gold, silver, cinnabar, lead, tin, copper, or other valuable deposits heretofore located, shall be governed as to length along the vein or lode by the customs, regulations, and laws in force at the date of their location. A mining-claim located after the passage of this act, whether located by one or more persons, may equal, but shall not exceed, one thousand and five hundred feet in length along the vein or lode; but no location of a mining-claim shall be made until the discovery of the vein or lode within the limits of the claim located. No claim shall extend more than three hundred feet on each side of the middle of the vein at the surface, nor shall any claim be limited by any mining regulation to less than twenty-five feet on each side of the middle of the vein at the surface, except where adverse rights existing at the passage of this act shall render such limitation necessary. The end-lines of each claim shall be parallel to each other.

An American flag marks a claim where miners collect necessary and valuable minerals.

SEC. 3. That the locators of all mining locations heretofore made, or which shall hereafter be made, on any mineral veln, lode, or ledge, situated on the public domain, their heirs and assigns, where no adverse claim exists at the passage of this act, so long as they comply with the laws of the United States, and with State, territorial, and local regulations not in conflict with said laws of the United States governing their possessory title, shall have the exclusive right of possession and enjoyment of all the surface included within the lines of their locations, and of all veins, lodes, and ledges throughout their entire clepth, the top or apex of which lies inside of such surface-lines extended downward vertically, although such veins, lodes, or ledges may so :far depart from a perpendicular in their course downward as to extend outside the vertical side-lines of said surface locations: Provided, That their right of possession to such outside parts of said veins or ledges shall be confined to such portions thereof as lie between vertical planes drawn downward as aforesaid, through the endlines of their locations. so continued in their own direction that such planes will intersect such exterior parts of said veins or ledges: And provided further, That nothing in this section shall authorize the locator or possessor of a vein or lode which extends in its downward course beyond the vertical lines of his claim to enter upon the surface of a claim owned or possessed by another.

SEC. 4. That where a tunnel is run for the development of a vein or lode, or for the discovery of mines, the owners of such tunnel shall have the right of possession of all veins or lodes within three thousand feet from the face of such tunnel on the line thereof not previously known to exist; discovered in such tunnel, to the same extent as if discovered from the surface; and locations on the line of such tunnel of veins or lodes not appearing on the surface, made by other parties after the commencement of the tunnel, and while the same is being prosecuted with reasonable diligence, shall be invalid; but failure to prosecute the work on the tunnel for six months shall be considered as an abandonment of the right to all undiscovered veins on the line of said tunnel.

A river in Idaho where a suction dredge miner works his legal, federal claim.

SEC. 5. That the miners of each mining district may make rules regulations not in conflict with the laws of the United States, or with the laws of the State or Territory in which the district is situated, governing the location, manner of recording, amount of work necessary to hold possession of a mining-claim, subject to the following requirements: The location must be distinctly marked on the ground so that its boundaries can be readily traced. All records of mining-claims hereafter made shall contain the name or names of the locators, the date of the location, and such a description of the claim or claims located by reference to some natural object or permanent monument as will identify the claim. On each claim located after the passage of this act, and until a patent shall have been issued therefore, not less than one hundred dollars' worth of labor shall be performed or improvements made during each year. On all claims located prior to the passage of this act, ten dollars' worth of labor shall be performed or improvements made each year for each one hundred feet in length along the vein until a patent shall have been issued therefore; but where such claims are held in common such expenditure may be made upon any one claim;, and upon a failure to comply with these conditions, the claim or mine upon which such failure occurred shall be open to relocation in the same manner as if no location of the same had ever been made: Provided, That the original locators, their heirs, assigns, or legal representatives, have not resumed work upon the claim after such failure and before such location. Upon the failure of any one of several co-owners to contribute his proportion of the expenditures required by this act, the co-owners who have performed the labor or made the improvements may, at the expiration of the year, give such delinquent co-owner personal notice in writing or notice by publication in the newspaper published nearest the claim, for at least once a week for ninety days, and if at the expiration of ninety days after such notice in writing or by publication such delinquent should fail or refuse to contribute his proportion to comply with this act his interest in the claim shall become the property of his co-owners who have made the required expenditures.

A miner rests on his small scale suction dredge in the middle of the river, on his claim. Fish love dredgers. They swarm to the waters near a dredge for a quick meal and hang around for more.

SEC. 6. That a patent for any land claimed and located for valuable deposits may be obtained in the following manner: Any person, association, or corporation authorized to locate a claim under this act, having claimed and located a piece of land for such purposes, who has or have complied with the terms of this act, may file in the proper land-office an application for a patent, under oath, showing such compliance, together with a plat and field-notes of the claim or claims in common, made by or under the direction of the United States surveyor-general, showing accurately the boundaries of the claim or claims, which shall be distinctly marked by monuments on the ground. and shall post a copy of such plat, together with a notice of such application for a patent, in a conspicuous place on the land embraced in such plat previous to the filing of the application for a patent, and shall file an affidavit of at least two persons that such notice has been duly posted as aforesaid, and shall file a copy of said notice in such land-office, and shall thereupon be entitled to a patent for said land, in the manner following: The register of the land-office, upon the filing of such application, plat, field-notes, notices, and affidavits, shall publish a notice that such application has been made, for the period of sixty days, in a newspaper to be by him designated as published nearest to said claim; and he shall also post such notice in his office for the same period. The claimant at the time of filing this application, or at any time thereafter, within the sixty days of publication, shall file with the register a certificate of the United States surveyor-general that five hundred dollars' worth of labor has been expended or improvements made upon the claim by himself or grantors; that the plat is correct, with such further description by such reference to natural objects or permanent monuments as shall identify the claim, and furnish an accurate description, to be incorporated in the patent. At the expiration of the sixty days of publication the claimant shall file his affidavit, showing that the plat and notice have been posted in a conspicuous place on the claim during said period of publication. If no adverse claim shall have been filed with the register and the receiver of the proper land-office at the expiration of the sixty days of publication, it shall be assumed that the applicant is entitled to a patent, upon the payment to the proper officer of five dollars per acre, and that no adverse claim exists ; and thereafter no objection from third parties to the issuance of a patent shall be heard, except it be shown that the applicant has failed to comply with this act.

A butterfly sits on a flower in a meadow in the Black Hills of South Dakota.

A beautiful section of the Fresno River in gold country. Coarsegold, CA.

SEC. 7. That where an adverse claim shall be filed during the period of publication, it shall be upon oath of the person or persons making the same, and shall show the nature, boundaries, and extent of such adverse is claim, and all proceedings, except the publication of notice and making and filing of the affidavit thereof; shall be stayed until the controversy shall have been settled or decided by a court of competent jurisdiction, or the adverse claim waived. It shall be the duty of the adverse claimant, within thirty days after filing his claim, to commence proceedings in a court of competent jurisdiction, to determine the question of the right of possession, and prosecute the same with reasonable diligence to final judgment; and a failure to do shall be a waiver of his adverse claim. After such judgment shall have been rendered, the party entitled to the possession of the claim, or any portion thereof may, without giving further notice, file a certified copy of the judgment-roll with the register of the land-office, together with the certificate of the surveyor-general that the requisite amount of labor has been expended, or improvements made thereon, and the description required in other cases, and shall pay to the receiver five dollars per acre for his claim, together with the proper fees, whereupon the whole proceedings and the judgment-roll shall be certified by the register to the commissioner of the general land office, and a patent shall issue thereon for the claim, or such portion thereof as the applicant shall appear, from the decision of the court, to rightly possess. If it shall appear from the decision of the court that several parties are entitled to separate, and different portions of the claim, each party may pay for his portion of the claim, with the proper fees, and file the certificate and description by the surveyor-general, whereupon the register shall certify the proceedings and judgment-roll to the commissioner of the general land office, as in the preceding case, and patents sball issue to the several parties according to their respective rights. Proof of citizenship under this act, or the acts of July twenty-sixth, eighteen hundred and sixty-six, and July ninth, eighteen hundred and seventy, in the case of an individual, may consist of his own affidavit thereof, and in case of an association of persons unincorporated, of the affidavit of their authorized agent, made on his own knowledge or upon information and belief, and in case of a corporation organized under the laws of the United States, or of any State or Territory of the United States, by the filing of a certified copy of their charter or certificate of incorporation; and nothing herein contained shall be construed to prevent the alienation of the title conveyed by a patent for a mining-claim to any person whatever.

Prospectors and miners have been finding gold in this river for more than 150 years and it still looks pristine.

SEC. 8. That the description of vein or lode claims, upon surveyed lands, shall designate the location of the claim with reference to the lines of the public surveys, but need not conform therewith; but where a patent shall be issued as aforesaid for claims upon unsurveyed lands, the surveyor-general, in extending the surveys, shall adjust the same to the boundaries of such patented claim, according to the plat or description thereof; but so as in no case to interfere with or change the location of any such patented claim.

SEC. 9. That sections one, two, three, four, and six of an act entitled "An act granting the right of way to ditch and canal owners over the public lands, and for other purposes," approved July twenty-sixth, eighteen-hundred and sixty-six, are hereby repealed, but such repeal shall not affect existing rights. Applications for patents for mining-claims now pending may be prosecuted to a final decision in the general land office; but in such cases where adverse rights are not affected thereby, patents may issue in pursuance of the provisions of this act; and all patents for mining-claims heretofore issued under the act of July twenty-sixth, eighteen hundred and sixty-six, shall convey all the rights and privileges conferred by this act where no adverse rights exist at the time of the passage of this act.

A miner's daughter, being raised right. She has an understanding of how important the earth is to her. Her parents are doing a good job of raising a responsible citizen.

Gold & mercury removed from a river by a miner.

SEC. 10. That the act entitled "An act to amend an act granting the right of way to ditch and canal owners over the public lands, and for other purposes," approved July ninth, eighteen hundred and seventy, shall be and remain in full force, except as to the proceedings to obtain a patent, which shall be similar to the proceedings prescribed by sections six and seven of this act for obtaining patents to vein or lode claims; but where said placer-claims shall be upon surveyed lands, and conform to legal subdivisions, no further survey or plat shall be required, and all placer mining-claims hereafter located shall conform as near as practicable with the United States system of public land surveys and the rectangular subdivisions of such surveys, and no such location shall include more than twenty acres for each individual claimant, but where such claims cannot be conformed to legal subdivisions, survey and plat shall be made as on unsurveyed lands: Provided, That proceedings now pending may be prosecuted to their final determination under existing laws; but the provisions of this act, when not in conflict with existing laws, shall apply to such cases: And provided also, That whereby the segregation of mineral land in any legal subdivision a quantity of agricultural land less than forty acres remains, said fractional portion of agricultural land may be entered by any party qualified by law, for homestead or pre-emption purposes.

SEC. 11. That where the same person, association, or corporation is in possession of a placer-claim, and also a vein or lode included within the boundaries thereof; application shall be made for a patent for the placer or lode claim, with the statement that it includes such vein or lode, and in such case (subject to the provisions of this act and the act entitled "An act to amend an act granting the right of way to ditch and canal owners over the public lands, and for other purposes," approved July eighteen hundred and seventy) a patent shall issue for the placer-claim, including such vein or lode, upon the payment of five dollars per acre for such vein or lode claim, and twenty-five feet of surface on each side thereof. The remainder of the placer-claim, or any placer-claim not embracing any vein or lode claim, shall be paid for at the rate of two dollars and fifty cents per acre, together with all costs of proceedings; and where a vein or lode, such as is described in the second section of this act, is known to exist within the boundaries of a placer-claim, all application for a patent for such placer-claim which does not include an application for the vein or lode claim shall be construed as a conclusive declaration that the claimant of the placer-claim has no right of possession but where the existence of a vein or lode in a placer-claim is not known, a patent for the placer-claim shall convey all valuable mineral and other deposits within the boundaries thereof.

It happens!

SBC. 12. That the surveyor-general of the United States may appoint in each land district containing mineral lands as many competent surveyors as shall apply for appointment to survey mining-claims. The expenses of the survey of vein or lode claims, and the survey and subdivision of placer-claims into smaller quantities than one hundred and sixty acres, together with the cost of publication of notices, shall be paid by the applicants, and they shall be at liberty to obtain the same at the most reasonable rates, and they shall also be at liberty to employ any United States deputy surveyor to make the survey. The commissioner of the general land office shall also have power to establish the maximum charges for surveys and publication notices under this act; and in case of excessive charges for publication, he may designate any newspaper published in a land district where mines are situated for the publication of mining-notices in such district, and fix the rates to be charged by such paper; and, to the end that the commissioner may be fully informed on the subject, each applicant shall file with the register a sworn statement of all charges and fees paid by said applicant for publication and surveys, Applicant to together with all fees and money paid the register and the receiver of the land-office, which statement shall be transmitted, with the other papers in the case, to the commissioner of the general land office. The fees of the register and the receiver shall be five dollars each for filing and acting upon each application for patent or adverse claim filed, and they shall be allowed the amount fixed by law for reducing testimony to writing, when done in the land-office, such fees and allowances to be paid by the respective parties; and no other fees shall be charged by them in such cases. Nothing in this act shall be construed to enlarge or affect the rights of either party in regard to any property in controversy at the time of the passage of this act, or of the act entitled "An act granting the right of way to ditch and canal owners over the public lands, and for other purposes," approved July twenty-sixth, eighteen hundred and sixty-six, nor shall this act affect any right acquired under said act; and nothing in this act shall be construed to repeal, impair, or in any way affect the provisions of the act entitled "An act granting to A. Sutro the right of way, and other privileges to aid in the construction of a draining and exploring tunnel to the Comstock lode, in the State of Nevada," approved July twenty-fifth, eighteen hundred and sixty-six.

A pan with beautiful gold in it. Gold is turned into electronic components, jewelry, coins, and more.

SEC. 13. That all affidavits required to be made under this act, or the act of which it is amendatory, may be verified before any officer authorized to administer oaths within the land-district where the claims may be situated, and all testimony and proofs may be taken before any such officer, and, when duly certified by the officer taking the same, shall have the same force and effect as if taken before the register and receiver of the land-office. In cases of contest as to the mineral or agricultural character of land, the testimony and proofs may be taken as herein provided on personal notice of at least ten days to the opposing party; or if said party cannot be found, then by publication of at least once a week for thirty days in a newspaper, to be designated by the register of the land-office as published nearest to the location of such land; and the register shall require proof that such notice has been given.

A dry California riverbed. All fish and other aquatic creatures are dead and gone. Miners didn't do this; Mother Nature did.

SEC. 14. That where two or more veins intersect or cross each other, priority of title shall govern, and such prior location shall be entitled to all ore or mineral contained within the space of intersection: Provided, however, That the subsequent location shall have the right of way through said space of intersection for the purposes of the convenient working of the said mine: And provided also, That where two or more veins unite, the oldest or prior location shall take the vein below the point of union, including all the space of intersection.

Our flag; symbol of freedom, symbol of strength.

SEC. 15. That where non-mineral land not contiguous to the vein or lode is used or occupied by the proprietor of such vein or lode for mining or milling purposes, such non-adjacent surface ground may be embraced and included in an application for a patent for such vein or lode, and the same may be patented therewith, subject to the same preliminary requirements as to survey and notice as are applicable under this act to veins or lodes: Provided, That no location hereafter made of such non-adjacent land shall exceed five acres, and payment for the same must be made at the same rate as hed by this act for the superficies of the lode. The owner ot a quartz-mill or reduction-works, not owning a mine in connection therewith, may also receive a patent for his mill-site, as provided in this section.

Miners are aware of invasive species in our waterways. A dialog free from fear is necessary between us and state biologists, who need to know about these and other harmful plants and animals.

SEO. 16. That all acts and parts of acts inconsistent herewith are hereby repealed: Provided, That nothing contained in this act shall be construed to impair, in any way, rights or interests in mining property acquired under existing laws.

APPROVED, May 10, 1872.

This is our way of helping you know your rights as a miner in the USA. Too many don't realize the US Constitution & US Congress are both on their side.

Knowledge is power and we are all about both for all miners in this great nation.

Please help us get the word out to miners everywhere by logging onto our website and supporting us.

www.americanminingrights.com